Some Imagist Poets: An Anthology

Amy Lowell, DH Lawrence, HD, etc

Some Imagist Poets: An Anthology

Table of Contents

Some Imagist Poets: An Anthology 1
    Amy Lowell, DH Lawrence, HD, etc. 1
Richard Aldington 2
    Childhood 3
    The Poplar 7
    Round–Pond 8
    Daisy 9
    Epigrams 10
    The Faun Sees Snow for the First Time 11
    Lemures 12
H.D. 12
    The Pool 13
    The Garden 13
    Sea Lily 14
    Sea Iris 15
    Sea Rose 16
    Oread 17
    Orion Dead 17
John Gould Fletcher 18
    The Blue Symphony 18
    London Excursion 22
F.S. Flint 30
    Trees 30
    Lunch 31
    Malady 32
    Accident 33
    Fragment 34
    Houses 35
    Eau–Forte 36
D.H. Lawrence 37
    Ballad of Another Ophelia 37
    Illicit 38
    Fireflies in the Corn 39
    A Woman and Her Dead Husband 40
    The Mowers 42

Some Imagist Poets: An Anthology

Table of Contents

Some Imagist Poets: An Anthology
- Scent of Irises...43
- Green..44

Amy Lowell..45
- Venus Transiens...45
- The Travelling Bear...46
- The Letter...46
- Grotesque...47
- Bullion..48
- Solitaire..48
- The Bombardment...49

Some Imagist Poets: An Anthology

Amy Lowell, DH Lawrence, HD, etc

Kessinger Publishing reprints thousands of hard-to-find books!

Visit us at http://www.kessinger.net

- Richard Aldington
    - Childhood
    - The Poplar
    - Round-Pond
    - Daisy
    - Epigrams
    - The Faun Sees Snow for the First Time
    - Lemures

- H.D.
    - The Pool
    - The Garden
    - Sea Lily
    - Sea Iris
    - Sea Rose
    - Oread
    - Orion Dead

- John Gould Fletcher
    - The Blue Symphony
    - London Excursion

Some Imagist Poets: An Anthology

- F.S. Flint
    - Trees
    - Lunch
    - Malady
    - Accident
    - Fragment
    - Houses
    - Eau–Forte

- D.H. Lawrence
    - Ballad of Another Ophelia
    - Illicit
    - Fireflies in the Corn
    - A Woman and Her Dead Husband
    - The Mowers
    - Scent of Irises
    - Green

- Amy Lowell
    - Venus Transiens
    - The Travelling Bear
    - The Letter
    - Grotesque
    - Bullion
    - Solitaire
    - The Bombardment

Richard Aldington

Childhood

I

THE bitterness. the misery, the wretchedness of childhood
Put me out of love with God.
I can't believe in God's goodness;
I can believe
In many avenging gods.
Most of all I believe
In gods of bitter dullness,
Cruel local gods
Who scared my childhood.

II

I've seen people put
A chrysalis in a match-box,
"To see," they told me, "what sort of moth would come."
But when it broke its shell
It slipped and stumbled and fell about its prison
And tried to climb to the light
For space to dry its wings.

That's how I was.
Somebody found my chrysalis
And shut it in a match-box.
My shrivelled wings were beaten,
Shed their colours in dusty scales
Before the box was opened
For the moth to fly.

III

Some Imagist Poets: An Anthology

I hate that town;
I hate the town I lived in when I was little;
I hate to think of it.
There wre always clouds, smoke, rain
In that dingly little valley.
It rained; it always rained.
I think I never saw the sun until I was nine —
And then it was too late;
Everything's too late after the first seven years.

The long street we lived in
Was duller than a drain
And nearly as dingy.
There were the big College
And the pseudo-Gothic town-hall.
There were the sordid provincial shops —
The grocer's, and the shops for women,
The shop where I bought transfers,
And the piano and gramaphone shop
Where I used to stand
Staring at the huge shiny pianos and at the pictures
Of a white dog looking into a gramaphone.

How dull and greasy and grey and sordid it was!
On wet days — it was always wet —
I used to kneel on a chair
And look at it from the window.

The dirty yellow trams
Dragged noisily along
With a clatter of wheels and bells
And a humming of wires overhead.
They threw up the filthy rain-water from the hollow lines
And then the water ran back
Full of brownish foam bubbles.

There was nothing else to see —
It was all so dull —
Except a few grey legs under shiny black umbrellas
Running along the grey shiny pavements;
Sometimes there was a waggon
Whose horses made a strange loud hollow sound
With their hoofs
Through the silent rain.

And there was a grey museum
Full of dead birds and dead insects and dead animals
And a few relics of the Romans — dead also.
There was a sea-front,
A long asphalt walk with a bleak road beside it,
Three piers, a row of houses,
And a salt dirty smell from the little harbour.

I was like a moth —
Like one of those grey Emperor moths
Which flutter through the vines at Capri.
And that damned little town was my match-box,
Against whose sides I beat and beat
Until my wings were torn and faded, and dingy
As that damned little town.
IV

At school it was just as dull as that dull High Street.
The front was dull;
The High Street and the other street were dull —
And there was a public park, I remember,
And that was damned dull, too,
With its beds of geraniums no one was allowed to pick,
And its clipped lawns you weren't allowed to walk on,
And the gold-fish pond you mustn't paddle in,
And the gate made out of a whale's jaw-bones,
And the swings, which were for "Board-School children,"

And its gravel paths.

And on Sundays they rang the bells,
From Baptist and Evangelical and Catholic churches.
They had a Salvation Army.
I was taken to a High Church;
The parson's name was Mowbray,
"Which is a good name but he thinks too much of it —"
That's what I heard people say.

I took a little black book
To that cold, grey, damp, smelling church,
And I had to sit on a hard bench,
Wriggle off it to kneel down when they sang psalms
And wriggle off it to kneel down when they prayed,
And then there was nothing to do
Except to play trains with the hymn-books.

There was nothing to see,
Nothing to do,
Nothing to play with,
Except that in an empty room upstairs
There was a large tin box
Containing reproductions of the Magna Charta,
Of the Declaration of Independence
And of a letter from Raleigh after the Armada.
There were also several packets of stamps,
Yellow and blue Guatemala parrots,
Blue stags and red baboons and birds from Sarawak,
Indians and Men-of-war
From the United States,
And the green and red portraits
Of King Francobello
Of Italy.

V

I don't believe in God.
I do believe in avenging gods
Who plague us for sins we never sinned
But who avenge us.

That's why I'll never have a child,
Never shut up a chrysalis in a match-box
For the moth to spoil and crush its brght colours,
Beating its wings against the dingy prison-wall.

The Poplar

WHY do you always stand there shivering
Between the white stream and the road?

The people pass through the dust
On bicycles, in carts, in motor-cars;
The waggoners go by at down;
The lovers walk on the grass path at night.

Stir from your roots, walk, poplar!
You are more beautiful than they are.

I know that the white wind loves you,
Is always kissing you and turning up
The white lining of your green petticoat.
The sky darts through you like blue rain,
And the grey rain drips on your flanks
And loves you.
And I have seen the moon
Slip his silver penny into your pocket

As you straightened your hair;
And the white mist curling and hesitating
Like a bashful lover about your knees.

I know you, poplar;
I have watched you since I was ten.
But if you had a little real love,
A little strength,
You would leave your nonchalant idle lovers
And go walking down the white road
Behind the waggoners.

There are beautiful beeches down beyond the hill.
Will you always stand there shivering?

Round–Pond

WATER ruffled and speckled by galloping wind
Which puffs and spurts it into tiny pashing breaks
Dashed with lemon–yellow afternoon sunlight.
The shining of the sun upon the water
Is like a scattering of gold crocus–petals
In a long wavering irregular flight.

The water is cold to the eye
As the wind to the cheek.

In the budding chestnuts

Whose sticky buds glimmer and are half-burst open
The starlings make their clitter-clatter;
And the blackbirds in the grass
Are getting as fat as the pigeons.

Too-hoo, this is brave;
Even the cold wind is seeking a new mistress.

Daisy

"Plus quan se atque suos amavit omnes,
nunc . . ."
        CATULLUS

YOU were my playmate by the sea.
We swam together.
Your girl's body had no breasts.

We found prawns among the rocks;
We liked to feel the sun and to do nothing;
In the evening we played games with the others.

It made me glad to be by you.

Sometimes I kissed you,
And you were always glad to kiss me;
But I was afraid — I was only fourteen.

And I had quite forgotten you,
You and your name.

To-day I pass through the streets.

She who touches my arms and talks with me
Is — who knows? — Helen of Sparta,
Dryope, Laodamia . . . .

And there are you
A whore in Oxford Street.

Epigrams

A Girl

YOU were that clear Sicilian fluting
That pains our thought even now.
You were the notes
Of cold fantastic grief
Some few found beautiful.
New Love

She had new leaves
After her dead flowers,
Like the little almond-tree
Which the frost hurt.
October

The beech-leaves are silver
For lack of the tree's blood.

At your kiss my lips
Become like the autumn beech-leaves.

The Faun Sees Snow for the First Time

ZEUS,
Brazen–thunder–hurler,
Cloud–whirler, son–of–Kronos,
Send vengeance on these Oreads
Who strew
White frozen flecks of mist and cloud
Over the brown trees and the tufted grass
Of the meadows, where the stream
Runs black through shining banks
Of bluish white.

Zeus,
Are the halls of heaven broken up
That you flake down upon me
Feather–strips of marble?

Dis and Styx!
When I stamp my hoof
The frozen–cloud–specks jam into the cleft
So that I reel upon two slippery points . . . .

Fool, to stand here cursing
When I might be running!

Lemures

IN Nineveh
And beyond Nineveh
In the dusk
They were afraid.

In Thebes of Egypt
In the dust
They chanted of them to the dead.

In my Lesbos and Achaia
Where the God dwelt
We knew them.

Now men say "They are not":
But in the dusk
Ere the white sun comes —
A gay child that bears a white candle —
I am afraid of their rustling,
Of their terrible silence,
The menace of their secrecy.

H.D.

The Pool

ARE you alive?
I touch you.
You quiver like a sea–fish.
I cover you with my net.
What are you — banded one?

The Garden

I

YOU are clear,
O rose, cut in rock,
hard as the descent of hail.

I could scrape the colour
from the petal,
like spilt dye from a rock.

If I could break you
I could break a tree.

If I could stir
I could break a tree,
I could break you.

II

O wind,

rend open the heat,
cut apart the heat,
rend it sideways.

Fruit can not drop
through this thick air:
fruit can not fall into heat
that presses up and blunts
the points of pears
and rounds the grapes.

Cut the heat,
plough through it,
turning it on either side
of your path.

Sea Lily

REED,
slashed and torn,
but doubly rich —
such great heads as yours
drift upon temple–steps,
but you are shattered
in the wind.

Myrtle–bark
is flecked from you,
scales are dashed from your stem
sand cuts your petal,
furrows it with hard edge,
like flint

on a bright stone.

Yet though the whole wind
slash as your bark,
you are lifted up,
aye — though it hiss
to cover you with froth.

Sea Iris

I

WEED, moss–weed,
root tangled in sand,
sea–iris, brittle flower,
one petal like a shell
is broken,
and you print a shadow
like a thin twig.

Fortunate one,
scented and stinging,
rigid myrrh–bud,
camphor–flower,
sweet and salt — you are wind
in our nostrils.

II

Do the murex–fishers
drench you as they pass?
Do your root drag up colour

from the sand?
Have they slipped gold under you;
rivets of gold?

Band of iris-flowers
above the waves,
You are painted blue,
painted like a fresh prow
stained among the salt weeds.

Sea Rose

ROSE, harsh rose,
marred and with stint of petals,
meagre flower, thin,
sparse of leaf,

more precious
than a wet rose,
single on a stem —
you are caught in the drift.

Stunted, with small leaf,
you are flung on the sands,
you are lifted
in the crisp sand
that drives in the wind.

Can the spice-rose
drip such acrid fragrance
hardened in a leaf?

Oread

WHIRL up, sea —
Whirl your pointed pines,
Splash your great pines
On our rocks,
Hurl your green over us,
Cover us with your pools of fir.

Orion Dead

[Artemis speaks]

THE cornel–trees
uplift from the furrows,
the roots at their bases
strike lower through the barley–sprays.

So arise and face me.
I am poisoned with the rage of song.

I once pierced the flesh
of the wild–deer,
now am I afraid to touch
the blue and the gold–veined hyacinths?

I will tear the full flowers
and the little heads
of the grape–hyacinths.

I will strip the life from the bulb
until the ivory layers
lie like narcissus petals
on the black earth.

Arise,
lest I bend an ash-tree
into a taut bow,
and slay — and tear
all the roots from the earth.

The cornel-wood blazes
and strikes through the barley-sprays,
but I have lost heart for this.

I break a staff.
I break the tough branch.
I know no light in the woods.
I have lost pace with the winds.

John Gould Fletcher

The Blue Symphony

I

THE darkness rolls upward.
The thick darkness carries with it

Some Imagist Poets: An Anthology

Rain and a ravel of cloud.
The sun comes forth upon earth.

Palely the dawn
Leaves me facing timidly
Old gardens sunken:
And in the gardens is water.

Sombre wrecks — autumnal leaves;
Shadowy roofs
In the blue mist,
And a willow–branch that is broken.

O old pagodas of my soul, how you glittered across green trees!
Blue and cool:
Blue, tremulously,
Blow faint puffs of smoke
Across sombre pools.
The damp green smell of rotted wood;
And a heron that cries from out the water.

II

Through the upland meadows
I go alone.
For I dreamed of someone last night
Who is waiting for me.

Flower and blossom, tell me do you know of her?

Have the rocks hidden her voice?
They are very blue and still.

Long upward road that is leading me,
Light hearted I quit you,
For the long loose ripples of the meadow–grass

Invite me to dance upon them.

Quivering grass
Daintily poised
For her foot's tripping.

O blown clouds, could I only race up like you,
Oh, the last slopes that are sun-drenched and steep!

Look, the sky!
Across black valleys
Rise blue-white aloft
Jagged, unwrinkled mountains, ranges of death.

Solitude. Silence.

III

One chuckles by the brook for me:
One rages under the stone.
One makes a spout of his mouth,
One whispers — one is gone.

One over there on the water
Spreads cold ripples
For me
Enticingly.

The vast dark trees
Flow like blue veils
Of tears
Into the water.

Sour sprites,
Moaning and chuckling,
What have you hidden from me?

"In the palace of the blue stone she lies forever
Bound hand and foot."

Was it the wind
That rattled the reeds together?

Dry reeds, a faint shiver in the grasses.

IV

On the left hand there is a temple:
And a palace on the right–hand side.
Foot–passengers in scarlet
Pass over the glittering tide.

Under the bridge
The old river flows
Low and monotonous
Day after day.

I have heard and have seen
All the news that has been:
Autumn's gold and Spring's green!

Now in my palace
I see foot-passengers
Crossing the river:
Pilgrims of Autumn
In the afternoons.

Lotus pools:
Petals in the water.
Such are my dreams.

For me silks are outspread.

I take my ease, unthinking.

V

And now the lowest pine-branch
Is drawn across the disk of the sun.
Old friends who will forget me soon
I must go on,
Towards those blue death-mountains
I have forgot so long.

In the marsh grasses
There lies forever
My last treasure,
With the hope of my heart.

The ice is glazing over.
Torn lanterns flutter,
On the leaves is snow.

In the frosty evening
Toll the old bell for me
Once, in the sleepy temple.

Perhaps my soul will hear.

Afterglow:
Before the stars peep
I shall creeep out into darkness.

London Excursion

'Bus

GREAT walls of green,
City that is afar.

We gallop along
Alert and penetrating,
Roads open about us,
Housetops keep at a distance.

Soft–curling tendrils,
Swim backwards from our image:
We are a red bulk,
Projecting the angular city, in shadows, at our feet.

Black coarse–squared shapes,
Hump and growl and assemble.
It is the city that takes us to itself,
Vast thunder riding down strange skies.

An arch under which we slide
Divides our lives for us:
After we have passed it
We know we have left something behind
We shall not see again.

Passivity,
Gravity,
Are changed into hesitating, clanking pistons and wheels.
The trams come whooping up one by one,
Yellow pulse–beats spreading through darkness.

Music–hall posters squall out:
The passengers shrink together,
I enter indelicately into all their souls.

It is a glossy skating rink,

On which winged spirals clasp and bend eath other:
And suddenly slide backwards towards the centre,
After a too–brief release.

A second arch is a wall
To separate our souls from rotted cables
Of stale greenness.

A shadow cutting off the country from us,
Out of it rise red walls.

Yet I revolt: I bend, I twist myself,
I curl into a million convolutions:
Pink shapes without angle,
Anything to be soft and woolly,
Anything to escape.

Sudden lurch of clamours,
Two more viaducts
Stretch out red yokes of steel,
Crushing my rebellion.

My soul shrieking
Is jolted forwards by a long hot bar —
Into direct distances.
It pierces the small of my back.
Approach

ONLY this morning I sang of roses;
Now I see with a swift stare,
The city forcing up through the air
Black cubes close piled and some half–crumbling over.

My roses are battered into pulp:
And there swells up in me
Sudden desire for something changeless,

Some Imagist Poets: An Anthology

Thrusts of sunless rock
Unmelted by hissing wheels.
Arrival

The rest is too still.

It is a red sea
Licking
The housefronts.

They quiver gently
From base to summit.
Ripples of impulse run through them,
Flattering resistance.

Soon they will fall;
Already smoke yearns upward.
Clouds of dust,
Crash of collapsing cubes.

I prefer deeper patience,
Monotony of stalled beasts.
O angle–builders,
Vainly have you prolonged your effort,
For I descend amid you,
Past rungs and slopes of curving slippery steel.
Walk

Sudden struggle for foothold on the pavement,
Familiar ascension.

I do not heed the city any more,
It has given me a duty to perform.
I pass along nonchalantly,
Insinuating myself into self–baffling movements.
Impalpable charm of back streets

Some Imagist Poets: An Anthology

In which I find myself:
Cool spaces filled with shadow.
Passers–by, white hammocks in the sunlight.

Bulging outcrush into old tumult;
Attainment, as of a narrow harbour,
Of some shop forgotten by traffic
With cool–corridored walls.
'Bus–Top

Black shapes bending
Taxicabs crush in the crowd.
The tops are each a shining square
Shuttles that steadily press through woolly fabric.

Drooping blossom,
Gas–standards over
Spray out jingling tumult
Of white–hot rays.
Monotonous domes of bowler–hats
Vibrate in the heat.

Silently, easily we sway through braying traffic,
Down the crowded street.
The tumult crouches over us,
Or suddenly drifts to one side.
Transposition

I am blown like a leaf
Hither and thither.
The city about me
Resolves itself into sound of many voices,
Rustling and fluttering,
Leaves shaken by the breeze.

A million forces ignore me, I know not why,

I am drunken with it all.
Suddenly I feel an immense will
Stored up hither to and unconscious till this instant.
Projecting my body
Across a streeet, in the face of all its traffic.

I dart and dash:
I do not know why I go.
These people watch me,
I yield them my adventure.

Lazily I lounge through labyrintine corridors,
And with eyes suddenly altered,
I peer into an office I do not know,
And wonder at a startled face that penetrates my own.

Roses — pavement —
I will take all this city away with me —
People — uproar — the pavement jostling and flickering —
Women with incredible eyelids:
Dandies in spats:
Hard-faced throng discussing me — I know them all.
I will take them away with me,
I insistently rob them of their essence,
I must have it all before night,
To sing amid my green.

I glide out unobservant
In the midst of the traffic
Blown like a leaf
Hither and thither,
Till the city resolves itself into the clamour of voices,
Crying hollowly, like the wind rustling through the forest
Against the frozen housefronts:
Lost in the glitter of a million movements.
Peripeteia

Some Imagist Poets: An Anthology

I can no longer find a place for myself:
I go.

There are too many things to detain me,
But the force behind is reckless.

Noise, uproar, movement
Slide me outwards,
Black sleet shivering
Down red walls.

In thick jungles of green, this gyration,
My centrifugal folly,
Through roaring dust and futility spattered,
Will find its own repose.

Golden lights will gleam sullenly into silence,
Before I return.
Mid–Flight

We rush, a black throng,
Straight upon darkness:
Motes scattered
By the arc's rays.

Over the bridge fluttering,
It is theatre–time,
No one heeds.

Lost amid greenness
We will sleep all night;
And in the morning
Coming forth, we will shake wet wings
Over the settled dust of to–day.

Some Imagist Poets: An Anthology

The city hurls its cobbled streets after us,
To drive us faster.

We must attain the night
Before endless processions
Of lamps
Push us back.
A clock with quivering hands
Leaps to the trajectory−angle of our departure.

We leave behind pale traces of achievement:
Fires that we kindled but were too tired to put out,
Broad gold fans brushing softly over dark walls,
Stifled uproar of night.

We are already cast forth:
The signal of our departure
Jerks down before we have learned we are to go.
Station

We descend
Into a wall of green.
Straggling shapes:
Afterwards none are seen.

I find myself
Alone.
I look back:
The city has grown.

One grey wall
Windowed, unlit.

Heavily, night
Crushes the face of it.

I go on.
My memories freeze
Like birds' cry
In hollow trees.

I go on.
Up and outright
To the hostility
Of night.

F.S. Flint

Trees

ELM trees
and the leaf the boy in me hated
long ago —
rough and sandy.

Poplars
and their leaves,
tender, smooth to the fingers,
and a secret in their smell
I have forgotten.

Oaks
and forest glades,
heart aching with wonder, fear:

their bitter mast.

Willows
and the scented beetle
we put in our handkerchiefs;
and the roots of one
that spread into a river:
nakedness, water and joy.

Hawthorn,
white and odorous with blossom,
framing the quiet fields,
and swaying flowers and grasses,
and the hum of bees.

Oh, these are the things that are with me now,
in the town;
and I am grateful
for this minute of my manhood.

Lunch

FRAIL beauty,
green, gold and incandescent whiteness,
narcissi, daffodils,
you have brought me Spring and longing,
wistfulness,
in your irradiance.

Therefore, I sit here
among the people,
dreaming,

and my heart arches
with all the hawthorn blossom,
the bees humming,
the light wind upon the poplars,
and your warmth and your love
and your eyes . . .
they smile and know me.

Malady

I MOVE:
perhaps I have wakened;
this is a bed;
this is a room;
and there is light . . .

Darkness!

Have I performed
the dozen acts or so
that make me the man
men see?

The door opens,
and on the landing —
quiet!
I can see nothing: the pain, the weariness!

Stairs, banisters, a handrail:
all indistinguishable.
One step farther down or up,
and why?

But up is harder. Down!
Down to this white blur;
it gives before me.

Me?

I extend all ways:
I fit into the walls and they pull me.

Light?

Light! I know it is light.

Stillness, and then,
something moves:
green, oh green, dazzling lightning!
And joy! this is my room;
there are my books, there the piano,
there the last bar I wrote,
there the last line,
and oh the sunlight!

A parrot screeches.

Accident

DEAR one!
you sit there
in the corner of the carriage;
and you do not know me;
and your eyes forbid.

Is it the dirt, the squalor,
the wear of human bodies,
and the dead faces of our neighbours?
These are but symbols.

You are proud; I praise you;
your mouth is set; you see beyond us;
and you see nothing.

I have the vision of your calm, cold face,
and of the black hair that waves above it;
I watch you; I love you;
I desire you.

There is a quiet here
within the thud–thud of the wheels
upon the railway.

There is a quiet here
within my heart,
but tense and tender . . .

This is my station . . .

Fragment

    . . . THAT night I loved you
in the candlelight.
Your golden hair
strewed the sweet whiteness of the pillows
and the counterpane.
O the darkness of the corners,

the warm air, and the stars
framed in the casement of the ships' lights!
The waves lapped into the harbour;
the boats creaked;
a man's voice sang out on the quay;
and you loved me.
In your love were the tall tree fuchsias,
the blue of the hortensias, the scarlet nasturtiums,
the trees on the hills,
the roads we had covered,
and the sea that had borne your body
before the rock of Hartland.
You loved me with these
and with the kindness of people,
country folk, sailors and fisherman,
and the old lady who had lodged us and supped us.
You loved me with yourself
that was these and more,
changed as the earth is changed
into the bloom of flowers.

Houses

EVENING and quiet:
a bird trills in the poplar trees
behind the house with the dark green door
across the road.

Into the sky,
the red earthenware and the galvanised iron chimneys
thrust their cowls.
The hoot of the steamers on the Thames is plain.

No wind;
the trees merge, green with green;
a car whirs by;
footsteps and voices take their pitch
in the key of dusk,
far-off and near, subdued.

Solid and square to the world
the houses stand,
their windows blocked with venetian blinds.

Nothing will move them.

Eau-Forte

ON black bare trees a stale cream moon
hangs dead, and sours the unborn buds.

Two gaunt old hacks, knees bent, heads low,
tug, tired and spent, an old horse tram.

Damp smoke, rank mist fill the dark square;
and round the bend six bullocks come.

A hobbling, dirt-grimed drover guides
their clattering feet to death and shame.

D.H. Lawrence

Ballad of Another Ophelia

OH, the green glimmer of apples in the orchard,
Lamps in a wash of rain,
Oh, the wet walk of my brown hen through the stackyard,
O, tears on the window pane!

Nothing now will ripen the bright green apples,
Full of disappointment and of rain,
Brackish they will taste, of tears, when the yellow dapples
Of Autumn tell the withered tale again.

All round the yard it is cluck, my brown hen,
Cluck, and the rain–wet wings,
Cluck, my marigold bird, and again
Cluck for your yellow darlings.

For the grey rat found the gold thirteen
Huddled away in the dark,
Flutter for a moment, oh the beast is quick and keen,
Extinct one yellow–fluffy spark.

. . . .

Once I had a lover bright like running water,
Once his face was laughing like the sky;
Open like the sky looking down in all its laughter
On the buttercups — and buttercups was I.

What then is there hidden in the skirts of all the blossom,
What is peeping from your wings, oh mother hen?
'Tis the sun who asks the question, in a lovely haste for wisdom —
What a lovely haste for wisdom is in men?

Yea, but it is cruel when undressed is all the blossom,
And her shift is lying white upon the floor,
That a grey one, like a shadow, like a rat, a thie, a rainstorm
Creeps upon her then and gathers in his store.

Oh, the grey garner that is full of half-grown apples,
Oh, the golden sparkles laid extinct — !
And oh, behind the cloud sheaves, like yellow autumn dapples,
Did you see the wicked sun that winked?

Illicit

IN front of the sombre mountains, a faint, lost ribbon of rainbow,
And between us and it, the thunder;
And down below, in the green wheat, the labourers
Stand like dark stumps, still in the green wheat.

You are near to me, and your naked feet in their sandals,
And through the scent of the balcony's naked timber
I distinguish the scent of your hair; so now the limber
Lightning falls from heaven.

Adown the pale-green, glacier-river floats
A dark boat through the gloom — and whither?
The thunder roars. But still we have each other.
The naked lightnings in the heaven dither

And disappear. What have we but each other?
The boat has gone.

Fireflies in the Corn

A Woman taunts her Lover

LOOK at the little darlings in the corn!
The rye is taller than you, who think yourself
So high and mighty: look how its heads are borne
Dark and proud in the sky, like a number of knights
Passing with spears and pennants and manly scorn.

And always likely! — Oh, if I could ride
With my head held high—serene against the sky
Do you think I'd have a creature like you at my side
With your gloom and your doubt that you love me?
O darling rye,
How I adore you for your simple pride!

And those bright fireflies wafting in between
And over the swaying cornstalks, just above
All their dark-feathered helmets, like little green
Stars come low and wandering here for love
Of this dark earth, and wandering all serene — !

How I adore you, you happy things, you dears
Riding the air and carrying all the time
Your little lanterns behind you: it cheers
My heart to see you settling and trying to climb
The cornstalks, tipping with fire their spears.

All over the corn's dim motion, against the blue
Dark sky of night, the wandering glitter, the swarm
Of questing brilliant things: — you joy, you true
Spirit of careless joy: ah, how I warm
My poor and perished soul at the joy of you!
The Man answers and she mocks

You're a fool, woman. I love you and you know I do!
— Lord, take his love away, it makes him whine.
And I give you everything that you want me to.
— Lord, dear Lord, do you think he ever can shine?

A Woman and Her Dead Husband

AH, stern cold man,
How can you lie so relentless hard
While I wash you with weeping water!
Ah, face, carved hard and cold,
You have been like this, on your guard
Against me, since death began.

You masquerader!
How can you shame to act this part
Of unswerving indifference to me?
It is not you; why disguise yourself
Against me, to break my heart,
You evader?

You've a warm mouth,
A good warm mouth always sooner to soften
Even than your sudden eyes.

Ah cruel, to keep your mouth
Relentless, however often
I kiss it in drouth.

You are not he.
Who are you, lying in his pace on the bed
And rigid and indifferent to me?
His mouth, though he laughed or sulked
Was always warm and red
And good to me.

And his eyes could see
The white moon hang like a breast revealed
By the slipping shawl of stars,
Could see the small stars tremble
As the heart beneath did wield
Systole, diastole.

And he showed it me
So, when he made his love to me;
And his brows like rocks on the sea jut out,
And his eyes were deep like the sea
With shadow, and he looked at me,
Till I sank in him like the sea,
Awfully.

Oh, he was multiform —
Which then was he among the manifold?
The gay, the sorrowful, the seer?
I have loved a rich race of men in one —
— But not this, this never-warm
Metal-cold — !

Ah, masquerader!
With your steel face white-enamelled
Were you he, after all, and I never

Saw you or felt you in kissing?
— Yet sometimes my heart was trammelled
With fear, evader!

You will not stir,
Nor hear me, not a sound.
— Then it was you —
And all this time you were
Like this when I lived with you.
It is not true,
I am frightened, I am frightened of you
And of everything.
O God! — God too
Has deceived me in everything,
In everything.

The Mowers

THERE'S four men mowing down by the river;
    I can hear the sound of the scythe strokes, four
Sharp breaths swishing: — yea, but I
    Am sorry for what's i' store.

The first man out o' the four that's mowin'
    Is mine: I mun claim him once for all:
— But I'm sorry for him, on his young feet, knowin'
    None o' the trouble he's led to stall.

As he sees me bringin' the dinner, he lifts
    His head as proud as a deer that looks
Shoulder–deep out o' th' corn: and wipes
    His scythe blade bright, unhooks

His scythe stone, an' over the grass to me!
    — Lad, tha's gotten a chilt in me,
An' a man an' a father tha'lt ha'e to be,
    My young slim lad, an' I'm sorry for thee.

Scent of Irises

A FAINT, sickening scent of irises
Persists all morning. Here in a jar on the table
A fine proud spike of purple irises
Rising above the clsss–room litter, makes me unable
To see the class's lifted and bended faces
Save in a broken pattern, amid purple and gold and sable.

I can smell the gorgeous bog–end, in its breathless
Dazzle of may–blobs, when the marigold glare overcast
You with fire on your brow and your cheeks and your chin as you dipped
Your face in your marigold bunch, to touch and contrast
Your own dark mouth with the bridal faint lady–smocks
Dissolved in the golden sorcery you should not outlast.

You amid the bog–end's yellow incantation,
You sitting in the cowslips of the meadows above,
  — Me, your shadow on the bog–flame, flowery may–bobs,
Me full length in the cowslips, muttering you love —
You, your soul like a lady–smock, lost, evanescent,
You, with your face all rich, like the sheen on a dove — !

You are always asking, do I remember, remember
The buttercup bog–end where the flowers rose up
And kindled you over deep with a coat of gold?

You ask again, do the healing days close up
The open darkness which then drew us in,
The dark that swallows all, and nought throws up.

You upon the dry, dead beech-leaves, in the fire of night
Burnt like a sacrifice; — you invisible —
Only the fire of darkness, and the scent of you!
— And yes, thank God, it still is possible
The healing days shall close the darkness up
Wherein I breathed you like a smoke or dew.

Like vapour, dew, or poison. Now, thank God,
The golden fire has gone, and your face is ash
Indistinguishable in the grey, chill day,
The night has burnt you out, at last the good
Dark fire burns on untroubled without clash
Of you upon the dead leaves saying me yea.

Green

THE sky was apple-green,
The sky was green wine held up in the sun,
The moon was a golden petal between.

She opened her eyes, and green
They shone, clear like flowers undone,
For the first time, now for the first time seen.

Amy Lowell

Venus Transiens

TELL me,
Was Venus more beautiful
Than you are,
When she topped
The crinkled waves,
Drifting shoreward
On her plaited shell?
Was Botticelli's vision
Fairer than mine;
And were the painted rosebuds
He tossed his lady,
Of better worth
Than the words I blow about you
To cover your too great loveliness
As with a gauze
Of misted silver?

For me,
You stand poised
In the blue and buoyant air,
Cinctured by bright winds,
Treading the sunlight.
And the waves which precede you
Ripple and stir
The sands at my feet.

The Travelling Bear

GRASS–BLADES push up between the cobblestones
And catch the sun on their flat sides
Shooting it back,
Gold and emerald,
Into the eyes of passers–by.
And over the cobblestones,
Square–footed and heavy,
Dances the trained bear.
The cobbles cut his feet,
And he has a ring in his nose
But still he dances,
For the keeper pricks him with a sharp stick,
Under his fur.
Now the crowd gapes and chuckles,
And boys and young women shuffle their feet in time to the dancing bear,
They see him wobbling
Against a dust of emerald and gold,
And they are greatly delighted.
The legs of the bear shake with fatigue
And his back aches,
And the shining grass–blades dazzle and confuse him.
But still he dances,
Because of the little, pointed stick.

The Letter

LITTLE cramped words scrawling all over the paper
Like draggled fly's legs,

What can you tell of the flaring moon
Through the oak leaves?
Or of my uncurtained window and the bare floor
Spattered with moonlight?
Your silly quirks and twists have nothing in them
Of blossoming hawthorns,
And this paper is dull, crisp, smooth, virgin of loveliness
Beneath my hand.
I am tired, Beloved, of chafing my heart against
The want of you;
Of squeezing it into little inkdrops,
And posting it.
And I scald alone, here, under the fire
Of the greater moon.

Grotesque

WHY do the lilies goggle their tongues at me
When I pluck them;
And writhe, and twist,
And stangle themselves against my fingers,
So that I can hardly weave the garland
For your hair?
Why do they shriek your name
And spit at me
When I would cluster them?
Must I kill them
To make them lie still,
And send you a wreath of lolling corpses
To turn putrid and soft
On your forehead
While you dance?

Bullion

MY thoughts
Chink against my ribs
And roll about like silver hail-stones.
I should like to spill them out,
And pour them, all shining,
Over you.
But my heart is shut upon them
And holds them straitly.
Come, You! and open my heart;
That my thoughts torment me no longer,
But glitter in your hair.

Solitaire

WHEN night drifts along the streets of the city,
And sifts down between the uneven roofs,
My mind begins to peek and peer.
It plays at ball in old, blue Chinese gardens,
And shakes wrought dice-cups in Pagan temples,
Amid the broken flutings of white pillars.
It dances with purple and yellow crocuses in its hair,
And its feet shine as they flutter over drenched grasses.
How light and laughing my mind is,
When all the good folk have put out their bed-room candles,
And the city is still!

The Bombardment

SLOWLY, without force, the rain drops into the city. It stops a moment on the carved head of Saint John, then slides on again, slipping and trickling over his stone cloak. It splashes from the lead conduit of a gargoyle, and falls from it in turmoil on the stones of the Cathedral square. Where are the people, and why does the fretted steeple sweep about in the sky? Boom! The sound swings against the rain. Boom, again! After it, only water rushing in the gutters, and the turmoil from the spout of the gargoyle. Silence. Ripples and mutters. Boom!

The room is damp, but warm. Little flashes swarm about from the firelight. The lustres of the chandelier are bright, and clusters of rubies leap in the bohemian glasses on the étagère. Her hands are restless, but the white masses of her hair are quite still. Boom! Will it never cease to torture, this iteration! Boom! The vibration shatters a glass on the étagère. It lies there formless and flowing, with all its crimson gleams shot out of pattern, spilled, flowing red, blood–red. A thin bell–note pricks through the silence. A door creaks. The old lady speaks: "Victor, clear away that broken glass." "Alas! Madame, the bohemian glass!" "Yes, Victor, one hundred years ago my father brought it — " Boom! The room shakes, the servitor quakes. Another goblet shivers and breaks. Boom!

It rustles at the window–pane, the smooth, streaming rain, and he is shut within its clash and murmur. Inside is his candle, his table, his ink, his pen, and his dreams. He is thinking, and the walls are pierced with beams of sunshine, slipping through young green. A fountain tosses itself up at the blue sky, and through the spattered water in the basin he can see copper carp, lazily floating among cold leaves. A wind–harp in the cedar-tree grieves and whispers, and words blow into his brain, bubbled, iridescent, shooting up like flowers of fire, higher and higher. Boom! The flame–flowers snap on their slender stems. The fountain rears up in long broken spears of disheveled water and flattens into the earth. Boom! And there is only the room, the table, the candle, and the sliding rain. Again, Boom! — Boom! — Boom! He stuffs his fingers into his ears. He sees corpses, and cries out in fright. Boom! It is night, and they are shelling the city! Boom! Boom!

A child wakes and is afraid, and weeps in the darkness. What has made the bed shake?

Some Imagist Poets: An Anthology

"Mother, where are you? I am awake." "Hush, my Darling, I am here." "But, Mother, something so queer has happened, the room shook." Boom! "Oh! What is it? What is the matter?" Boom! "Where is Father? I am so afraid." Boom! The child sobs and shrieks. The house trembles and creaks. Boom!

Retorts, globes, tubes, and phials lie shattered. All his trials oozing across the floor. The life that was his choosing, lonely, urgent, goaded by a hope, all gone. A weary gloom and ignorance, and the jig of drunken brutes. Diseases like snakes crawling over the earth, leaving trails of slime. Wails from people burying their dead. Through the window he can see the rocking steeple. A ball of fire falls on the lead of the roof, and the sky tears apart on the spike of flame. Up the spire, behind the lacings of stone, zig-zagging in and out of the carved tracings, squirms the fire. It spouts like yellow wheat from the gargoyles, coils round the head of Saint John, and aureoles him in light. It leaps into the night and hisses against the rain. The Cathedral is a burning stain on the white, wet night.

Boom! The Cathedral is a torch, and the houses next to it begin to scorch. Boom! The bohemian glass on the étagère is no longer there. Boom! A stalk of flame sways against the red damask curtains. The old lady cannot walk. She watches the creeping stalk and counts. Boom! — Boom! — Boom!

The poet rushes into the street, and the rain wraps him in a sheet of silver. But it is threaded with gold and powdered with scarlet beads. The city burns. Quivering, spearing, thrusting, lapping, streaming, run the flames. Over the roofs, and walls, and shops, and stalls. Smearing its gold on the sky the fire dances, lances itself through the doors, and lisps and chuckles along the floors.

The child wakes again and screams at the yellow petalled flower flickering at the window. The little red lips of flame creep along the ceiling beams.

The old man sits among his broken experiments and looks at the burning Cathedral. Now the streets are swarming with people. They seek shelter and crowd into the cellars. They shout and call, and over all, slowly and without force, the rain drops into the city. Boom! And the steeple crashes down among the people. Boom! Boom, again! The water rushes along the gutters. The fire roars and mutters. Boom!

Printed in the United States
105306LV00004B/104/A